CHIARA DAL CANTO
LORENZO PENNATI

SIGNATURE HOUSES

PRIVATE HOMES
BY GREAT ITALIAN
DESIGNERS

RIZZOLI
NEW YORK

New York · Paris · London · Milan

CONTENTS

THE FRAGILE HOME

This book explores ten exemplary interiors, revealing design themes, events, and figures that occupied the cultural scene in Italy during the second half of the twentieth century.

These are "manifesto" homes because they are singular and unique—some the expression of authoritative architects, others of major figures in the worlds of design and interior decoration.

Many were the homes of their designers. Interiors that narrate their lives: encounters, books, and habits. Character-houses, where the space and the person are one. Testaments to an age of research, experimentation, and new languages. There is something exciting about these houses, because they interweave the private dimension with the work created by those who lived there, as recorded in images that dwell on details, travel memoires, the most intimate stories. This is the case with the home of Gae Aulenti, a master architect.

There are those who, like Osvaldo Borsani, designed a very significant building, where the family story has written important pages in history and where private events have intertwined with stylistic themes and the evolution of craftsmanship toward industrial production.

Memories are layered in the interiors, and Alessandro Mendini has chosen an old Belle Époque villa, almost clashing with the verdant mountain valley of the Bergamasco, to relocate many of his works and create new ones. Likewise, Gabriella Crespi has left her heritage of inventions and originality within the walls of her home in Milan, where she lived for a long time before finding a second, spiritually rich, life in India.

In Barnaba Fornasetti's home, important artists met and here his father Piero expressed his creativity, which still seems inexhaustible, thanks to an archive built up with extreme precision, an endless source of magic. It seems as though we can still hear his voice through a sort of megaphone, giving instructions to his employees.

In the house where he spent his final years, Umberto Riva, a refined architect, epitomized his poetics by impressing his vision even on the most humdrum objects, such as the coat stand in yellow sheet metal—an iconic, elegant, and detailed object with the energy of a work of art.

Some of these homes were designed and furnished not for architects but for clients. Homes as total works of art, such as Casa Tabarelli by Carlo Scarpa and Sergio Los, where architecture, art, and design combine and create a dialogue through the space, which was devised in extraordinary synergy between the clients and the designers.

A shared aesthetic also gave rise to the apartment where Elena Quarestani lives. In the mid-1980s, she asked Ettore Sottsass to remodel her home in Milan, and ever since she has breathed the same atmosphere as if untouched by time, preserving a project that has not aged.

A place, Lake Garda, and an encounter with the artist and intellectual André Bloc underlie a masterpiece of Italian architecture: Villa La Scala, designed by Vittoriano Viganò, who realized the aspiration of making nature the protagonist and the home, a transparent fortress.

Finally, there is an interior that has never been inhabited. Today, expertly reconstructed and preserved, it contains all the elements of its desinger's vocabulary, the eccentric and mysterious Carlo Mollino, an architect from Turin who has left us with this enigma.

What unites ten homes—so diverse in genesis, period, and taste—is that they have been preserved because an enlightened owner, a lover of beauty, or sometimes generations that followed have succeeded in safeguarding them.

Because homes are, first and foremost, fragile.

The same is true of interior designs that have master designers, being erased without regard by a new owner or just the passage of time. Their lifespan is often very short, and it is surprising that the dominant culture, which views vintage furnishings and period pieces with such great interest, does not lavish the same care on the interiors that hosted those same objects.

A whole heritage of homes that have had authorial qualities and have left their mark on the evolution of styles are today documented only thanks to period photographs. This is true of some works by the architects present in this volume, including Umberto Riva and Carlo Mollino. The transience of interiors is accepted as their inevitable fate.

We are grateful to the owners and conservators of the homes photographed in this book for opening their doors and enabling us to offer a new photographic view of them.

Homes, like people, can be more or less photogenic apart from their beauty. A portrait, however, is said to be successful only when, in addition to the outward appearance, it captures the soul.

This also happens with interiors. We hope that it is the deep soul of the homes that emerges in these images, all previously unpublished.

CASA
RIGHI

CASA RIGHI
UMBERTO RIVA, MILAN, 2002

In a multilevel home, formerly a workshop, Riva includes the most significant aspects of his architectural language: a quest for asymmetry, a preference for sharp edges, custom-made furnishings, a decidedly painterly color palette, and a metal staircase that seems suspended in midair. A design from his later years, it is faithful to his poetics in which research is a constant.

Previous pages:
*Living room and kitchen, a single large
space furnished with pieces designed
by Umberto Riva.
The Lem lamp and, in the background,
a painting by Riva himself.*

*The Veronese lamp and a diagonal
colored partition.*

When Umberto Riva designed Casa Righi in
2002 he already had forty years of experience behind him and numerous exemplary
designs that would earn him the Gold Medal for Lifetime
Achievement at the Milan Triennale in 2018.

Known to be one of the most interesting architects
of the postwar period, Riva was an extremely private individual who shunned the social limelight and was deeply
loved and studied by those who appreciated the originality
of his work. He built extensively, but even more distinctive
were the apartments he designed over the years, devoting
himself above all to interiors together with numerous exhibition and product designs.

His works from the 1960s are widely studied in
schools of architecture: Casa Berrini at Taino, a villa with
distant origins in the Lombard farmhouses, and before
that his holiday homes at Stintino, which drew on the
stazzi in Sardinia, the home on Via Paravia in Milan, and
his final works in Salento. Nevertheless, Umberto Riva
continues to be unknown to the general public, a highly
original artist yet outside all trends, far from marginal but
rather quiet and less aligned.

Painting had profound meaning in his life. He practiced and studied it, not just because he had attended the
Brera Academy before becoming an architect, but out of
a deep understanding of the work of artists such as Pierre
Bonnard, Max Beckmann, and Constantin Brancusi, to
whom he dedicated his first lamp E63, and, among the
Italians, Osvaldo Licini and Arturo Martini. He never
followed the Milanese school of architects, such as Albini
and Gardella, though he admired it. "I've always thought
that it sinned in elegance, that it expressed too much of a
certain upper-bourgeois distinction." Getting to know the
work of Carlo Scarpa, when he moved to the university in

Venice to finish his studies, was very significant. "It taught the intensity of architecture. Even suffering."

A work from his final years, Casa Righi embodies some significant features of Riva's language, from which emerges a vision of design continuously subjected to the practice of pencil drawing, erased and then picked up again, a search for solutions that had to be verified on-site, and a very personal reinterpretation of individual elements in the vocabulary of architecture: internal partitions, windows, dividing elements, stairs, and furnishings.

"The apartments he put his hand to successfully," wrote Alberto Ferlenga, "reveal, after his intervention, something that they may have contained, but that only the gaze of a visionary architect could see even on the smallest scale." The words reflect Riva's own, seeing the act of designing "as a continuous encirclement of something that you know exists outside your own will."

Casa Righi is located in Milan, in a building once used as a workshop not far from the Navigli. The two floors (15 feet high) were the object of a refined makeover that created three levels. The upper one intended for the living area keeps the original height, while the lower one is divided into two floors. The layout of the intermediate level, which works on the diagonals, creates a bedroom that envisages an acute angle and through a small window it overlooks the lower floor, which rises to double height. A trapezoidal volume contains, almost suspended, the metal staircase connecting the three levels. On the lower floor, the large study of the client, a psychiatrist, is preceded by a waiting area that stands out for the presence of a coat rack in sheet metal painted yellow. This is a magnificent object that expresses all of Riva's aversion to right angles, preferring sharp or obtuse ones as dynamic elements, while the precision of its manufacture represents his respectful

relationship with craftsmen through dialogue and involvement in the project.

Double heights and the original concrete beams left exposed alternate with more intimate interiors, where the custom-designed furnishings and the colors of the walls create a surprising rhythm. The considerable work on the form of both spaces and objects here does not seek to express, just as in previous interiors, a sense of self-representation. Instead, complexity seems to be at the service of an intimate and shared domestic life.

In the apartments designed by Riva, the internal layout frequently contains decisive elements that create architecture-furnishings that serve to divide the interiors. They do not reach the ceiling, as is the case with portions of the walls, which allow the eye to admire the vault in its entirety.

Both devices are adopted to welcome the visitor into the entryway of Casa Righi. The furniture separating the entryway from the kitchen is a complex filter using different materials and colors. It offers a support surface with a trapezoidal shape resting on three tapering legs surmounted by a panel that seems suspended and houses a painted work. On the kitchen side, a wall unit in varnished sheet metal with sliding poplar panels occupies the upper part, and a small slit connects the two sides, allowing the gaze to range further. Opposite, a masonry block, consisting of walls with different patterns and colors, only nine feet high, conceals the service rooms and creates a sort of colored box that stands out from the neutral shades of the container.

"Instinctively, I have always favored asymmetrical forms," were Riva's own words. "I dislike symmetrical ones. I have always thought that asymmetry makes everything less stable, less secure, less precise, less affirmative.

The E63 lamp rests on the desktop of the partition cabinet and,
above, the shelf suspended over the fireplace holds an African sculpture and,
in the background, the Franceschina lamp.

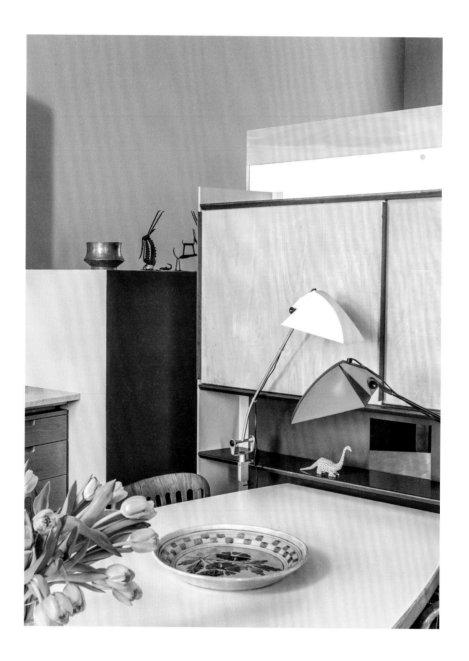

The convivial kitchen centers around a large table;
the partition is a small double-sided architectural furnishing with different functions on either front.
Right: *Above the table, the Sospesa lamp, and on the table, the E63 lamp.*

There is another thing that is part of my inspiration: precariousness. I dislike affirmation, certainty, and I always think everything is unstable."

An existential position that suggests an artistic practice rather than the art of building, an art that Riva constantly submits to revisions and doubts without allowing time to mitigate them. Casa Righi has also been a source of rethinking. In the long conversations online that Vitangelo Ardito and Nicoletta Faccitondo had with Riva during the pandemic (in 2020, one year before his death), now collected in the volume *Umberto Riva. Perciò è sempre una sorpresa*, he stated: "It may be that you can't bring some experiences to an end [. . .]. If I could now repaint Casa Righi, I would do it all in variations of white, white-beige, white-gray, with very few different shades. It is as if for me, today, the era of bold contrasts is over."

Riva lived for many years in this home, which bears traces of his presence—of the pictures he painted, the books he read, the objects he drew. Lamps, above all, glowing sculptures that from the E67 mentioned above, now back in production, are recognizable by their character as precious objects and by the precision of their details. In particular, those for Barovier&Toso: the sophisticated Veronese in very fine glass and brass details with birch inserts, which takes its name from Paolo Veronese's *Annunciation*, by which Riva was inspired, together with the models Tesa, Attesa,

and Sospesa, with the last of these over the kitchen table. Or Lem, with a resin glass clamp and diffuser, created for VeArt and then revised for the Galleria Antonia Jannone. Many of the furnishings are also designed—chairs, tables, and coffee tables, especially in wood—with forms typical of his language: oblique cuts, triangular shapes, thicknesses that shrink and look by assonance to designers such as Jean Prouvé and Pierre Chareau, whom Riva studied and admired. And again carpets, with delicate colors, which translate his paintings into textiles.

One final topic that should not be overlooked in trying to understand his work is exhibition design. They were numerous and of such high quality that they "prompt us to define Riva," wrote Gabriele Neri, "as one of the few heirs and continuators of that exceptional museographic tradition that in Italy, almost without interruption, was preceded by the Triennales of the 1930s until the 1960s, transforming the very notion of museums with exploits both large and small." With Frederick Kiesler, Palladio, Carlo Scarpa, John Soane, and Le Corbusier, among others, Riva engaged in a dialogue by designing exhibitions devoted to them in prestigious venues, always keeping alive his inclination to seek a balance in precariousness and transform details into important episodes.

"There is the architect-demiurge who knows, and the architect who does not know but wishes to. I belonged to this latter species."

View of the living room, a double-height space painted in shades of gray. On the floor, a carpet by Riva.

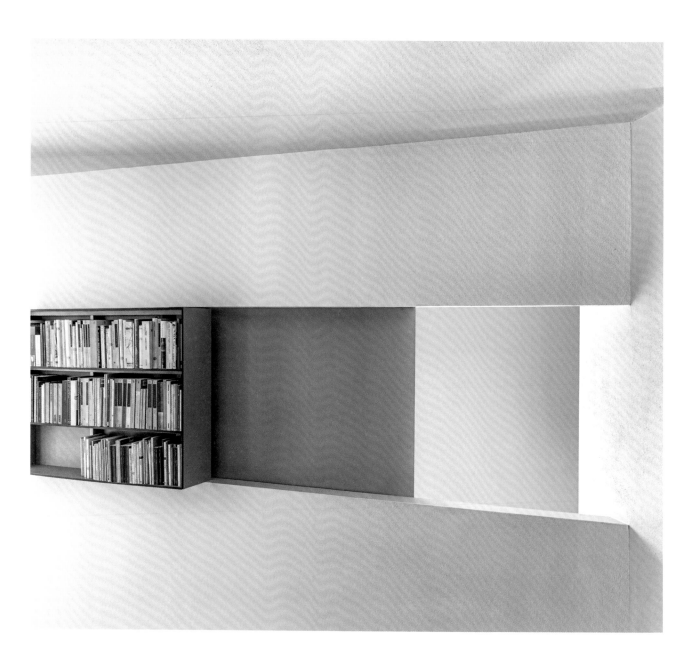

*The bedroom on the intermediate level overlooks the lower floor through
a horizontal opening incorporating a bookcase.*

From the lower-floor bedroom the rotated layout of the upper floor is noticeable and,
above, the trapezoidal window connecting the bedroom on the intermediate floor with the stairwell.

Previous pages, on the left: *Slits in the walls of the stairwell create an interplay of light.*
On the right: *Detail of the staircase connecting the three levels.*

In the entryway on the lower floor, the trapezoidal coat rack is accompanied by an armchair with an irregular silhouette.

Following pages: *The pass-through featuring oblique slits in the walls.*

CASA AULENTI

CASA AULENTI

GAE AULENTI, MILAN, SINCE 1974

The large space, dominated by a staircase with industrial overtones, is cluttered with objects, drawings, and prototypes of her work. Here one senses the layers of time and the memory of intellectual encounters and emotional relationships. Home and studio form a seamless whole, divided but contiguous, without any interruption between her personal and professional life.

To many she was *la Gae*, certainly to her friends—many and all belonging to a certain cultural milieu—and also to those who, without knowing it, thought of her as an important presence on Milan's intellectual scene. She was a point of reference, one of the few women architects who contributed to the prestige of the city without receiving frequent professional opportunities. Shortly after her death, Milan named a large piazza after her.

Gae, short for Gaetana, Aulenti was born in Veneto to a family whose roots lay in the South: Pugliese on her father's side and Calabrian on her mother's, both with intellectual roots and with magistrates, doctors, and academics in the family. She moved to Biella with her parents, where she took part in the Resistance at the age of fourteen. It may have been the sight of wartime rubble that prompted her to contribute to the rebirth. "Architecture was useful," in her own words, and it was one of the reasons that led her to enroll in the School of Architecture in Milan.

Looking at her long and complex career, in light of the statements she made, it is clear that the architect's character was strong and firmly rooted, and that she nurtured a genuine passion for architecture, which she practiced with iron discipline. "I've been lucky. I like my work and I really enjoy doing it. I love doing construction drawings, running a building site, watching a building grow. I like the smell of cement."

An eighteenth-century building overlooking Piazza San Marco hosts her home in Milan. Today, it holds the archive curated by her granddaughter Nina Artioli—who is also an architect—preserving all the records of her work for a total of more than 700 designs. On entering, you feel like you are encroaching on Gae Aulenti's proverbial reserve, in a place that is densely private, full of memories, mementos of travels, books, and encounters. In reality, home and studio have always been a single whole, divided yet contiguous, with her private and professional life seamlessly joined. Gae Aulenti moved here in the mid-1970s, and she liked to recall that between the walls of her studio, in a part of a building that protrudes from the facade, Giuseppe Verdi had composed his *Requiem*, performed for the first time in the Church of San Marco. She designed the interiors bearing her hallmark, taking advantage of the double-height ceiling with a staircase in red bearing industrial overtones that becomes a suspended walkway above the large, highly complex living room. At the top, you discover it from a new perspective, and from here you come to the terrace on one side, through a short veranda, and on the other, the guest quarters. It is a space where everything is connected, unlike bourgeois and ceremonial interiors. Here "social life unfolds in simple ways," she once said in an interview, "but this does not mean that they are not sophisticated." It is dominated by a large tapestry by Roy Lichtenstein ("a multiple of ten, otherwise I could never have afforded it"), cluttered with paintings, drawings, sculptures, and models of her architecture, and filled with specimens of the lamps she designed: the well-known Pipistrello and the Ruspa, both for Martinelli Luce; the King Sun, designed in 1967 for the Olivetti store in Paris and manufactured by Kartell; and Giova, in glass, designed for Fontana Arte, a historic brand of which Aulenti was director for many years. And her furnishings: the Sgarsul armchair for Poltronova, and the Locus Solus outdoor series, currently for Exteta, among others.

Everything is very natural but intensely expressive. You sense the layering of time, the memory of intellectual encounters and emotional relationships: Umberto Eco, Vittorio Gregotti, Luca Ronconi, Inge Feltrinelli, Emilio Tadini, and Maurizio Pollini were friends with whom she debated, worked, and shared her holidays.

After graduating in 1954, Aulenti joined the editorial staff of *Casabella*, a prestigious magazine edited by Ernesto Nathan Rogers for more than ten years, with his ideas influencing the "best of youth" among the architects of the time, including Vittorio Gregotti, Aldo Rossi, Guido Canella, and Giancarlo De Carlo.

In that all-male circle, probably also exclusive and not easy to gain entry to, Gae Aulenti was the only woman.

The question that arises from the combination of woman and architect in Aulenti's case goes straight to her own unhesitating clarification. "Although architecture is considered a man's craft," she said, "and being a woman may have harmed me, I pretend not to know it. I ignore it, because it could block my professional progress."

Action, practice as creed and civil commitment lavished on imagining a new structure of the city, of the single building and the objects within, were combined in her work with interdisciplinarity, the curiosity with which she studied and explored paths parallel to architecture. Art, first of all, by designing important exhibitions and creating museums, and then theatre, in partnership with Ronconi, who realized she was an exceptional set designer.

Her transversal interests and the desire to avoid specializing were qualities that broadened her professional boundaries in the name of coherence and a love of challenges. In them we recognize both the lesson of Ernesto Rogers—who invited architects to expand their range of observation—and a feminine quality that led "to the perception of things in depth rather than on the surface, and a preference for knowledge over power."

From early on in her career, she devoted herself to architectural, interior, and industrial designs, developing them along parallel lines and elaborating a vocabulary in which experimentation was important, going beyond the

Previous pages:
The large living room on two levels, notable for its system of stairways and walkways.

Detail of the rust-colored iron staircase and, above,
some mementos from Gae Aulenti's professional and private life.

constraints of Rationalism and interconnecting disciplines. She always remained a profound architect, even when she was designing a lamp, a theatrical space, or an interior. "My furnishings have always been interior architecture," she stated, "one architecture within another architecture."

In the 1960s, her commitment took on an international dimension thanks to important clients: Olivetti, for which she designed the showrooms in Paris and Buenos Aires, and Knoll International, with showrooms in Boston, New York, and later Milan. An important relationship developed over the years with Fiat, for which she designed numerous showrooms and installations in Turin, Geneva, Zurich, Brussels, and Vienna. From Gianni Agnelli came the request for her to design his private apartment in Milan, known as the House of the Collector through the photos by Ugo Mulas. Later, in the mid-1980s, she was commissioned to renovate Palazzo Grassi in Venice, where she designed the installations of some thirty exhibitions, the most prestigious ones. The theme of exhibition design was central to her profession and brought her into contact with avant-garde artists and curators like Germano Celant and Pontus Hultén.

In the mid-1970s, Luca Ronconi suggested she collaborate with the Laboratorio di Progettazione Teatrale in Prato. This resulted in memorable, wide-ranging productions: Alban Berg's *Wozzeck* conducted by Claudio Abbado at La Scala; Hugo von Hofmannsthal's play *Der turm*, for which she recreated the imperial palace of Würzburg within a former industrial space, the Fabbricone in Prato; Euripides's *Bacchantes* staged with a single actress, Marisa Fabbri, and twenty-four spectators at a time; and Gioachino Rossini's *La donna del lago*, which she directed herself with Maurizio Pollini conducting. And again, for Rossini's unforgettable *Viaggio a Reims*, she designed not only the sets but also the costumes. Gae Aulenti has left a profound mark in the history of Italian theatre, contributing decisively to a sucessful phase of great experimentation.

In 1980, her project for converting the Gare d'Orsay in Paris into a museum won an international competition and led to her breakthrough, giving Gae Aulenti visibility in the eyes of the world. The project lasted six years, with authoritative architecture for an exceptional collection that includes French art from the nineteenth century up to post-impressionism. The Musée d'Orsay was inaugurated by the then-president François Mitterrand in December 1986 and became an unmissable destination for millions of visitors. In her design, Gae Aulenti said she had conceived the architecture as subordinated to the artworks, while seeking as far as possible to preserve the beauty of Victor Laloux's building, though there were some criticisms of it. After all, her work does not seem to have been made to please everyone. Without indulging the public, it was its complexity that proved eloquent, together with a personal vision pursued through great determination.

Over the following years, other important museum designs followed: the Museu Nacional d'Art de Catalunya in Barcelona and the Asian Art Museum in San Francisco. Then came the Scuderie del Quirinale in Rome and the Italian Cultural Institute in Tokyo.

Her extensive output was created here, between home and studio, two spaces separated by an almost invisible door, with a team that was small compared to the size of the designs she dealt with, including the numerous competitions she took part in and for which, without winning them, she accepted some substantial challenges. Her character—determined, curious, cultured, and refined—imbues these spaces in Milan. As her daughter Giovanna, a famous theatrical costume designer, recalls, "in our family, affections have never been expressed in words but through places."

Previous page and above: *Many of the objects designed by Gae Aulenti
tell of her various collaborations.*

Right: *A sculpture by Fausto Melotti.*

Large bookcases form the backdrop to many rooms in her home-studio.
The design of the bed calls to mind the canopies in Giotto's paintings.

The King Sun lamp. Lighting, both natural and artificial,
was a key feature of Gae Aulenti's designs.

The combination of spaces between the apartment and the building in Piazza San Marco create a winter garden accessing the terrace. Here we find Locus Solus, one of her first systems of garden furniture.

CASA TABARELLI

CASA TABARELLI

CARLO SCARPA WITH SERGIO LOS, CORNAIANO, 1967

Amid vineyards surrounding Bolzano, architecture and nature establish an original dialogue in a villa whose design is determined by the alignment of the vine rows. Rooms with gardens, large windows facing the landscape, and a colorful origami-like ceiling are some of the features that make this location truly unique.

This is a home with a complex past, built in the mid-1960s amid the vineyards of Cornaiano, on the uplands near Bolzano. In a rural setting where the buildings are simple, repetitive, and mostly with pitched roofs, Casa Tabarelli clearly stands out. It does so quietly, not because the solutions adopted are not courageous but because it avoids asserting itself and is able to establish a dialogue with the surrounding landscape, to immerse itself and let itself be penetrated by it.

It is a building with different levels of interpretation. Refined inside, with an alternation of high-ceilinged spaces, large glazed areas, and rooms of a smaller size, it creates a constant relationship between interior and exterior, a sophisticated exploration of domesticity and nature.

The rows of vineyards running parallel, following the contours of the land and creating a precise natural geometry, are the source of its design. Casa Tabarelli is difficult to identify at a single glance, as normally happens with buildings set in the center of a garden. You approach expecting to see it, to pick it out among the others, but it escapes the eye. You discover it when you get up close and not even then in its entirety. You walk through the garden all around and it reveals itself piecemeal. Even its substantial roof does not allow itself to be perceived fully.

The design was conceived by Carlo Scarpa and was built by his student and colleague Sergio Los with significant input from the owners.

As Roberto Gigliotti, associate professor of Interior & Exhibit Design at the University of Bolzano, described in his essay *Casa Tabarelli. 1968-2008*: "The project can be considered a work by 'six hands': those of Carlo Scarpa—who, inspired by the spirit of the place, made a house for a collector and his family—those of Sergio Los—the creator of this project—and those of Gianni Tabarelli, who oversaw the construction personally and intervened directly, especially on the fixed furnishings, and in its realization fulfilled the dream of his partner Laura, who wanted a home in which to live with her family."

The clients, therefore, are significant. In the mid-1960s, Gianni Tabarelli de Fatis and his wife Laura were the owners of a furniture store in the center of Bolzano that offered the most innovative products from the world of design. Gianni was responsible for a major turning point in the family business, thanks to his curiosity, intellectual vivacity, and passion for art. His encounter with Dino Gavina—an influential figure in the field of design, an enlightened entrepreneur, furniture publisher, and founder of the company by the same name and later of Simon and Flos—proved decisive. He was a friend of Carlo Scarpa, some of whose furnishings he issued, making them very well known. In the early 1960s, Gavina asked Scarpa to design the store bearing his name in Bologna. And it was Gavina, a friend of Man Ray, Fontana, and Matta, who introduced Scarpa to the couple. "Toward the Professor," recalls his wife in conversation with Roberto Gigliotti, "Gianni felt a form of reverence. So I had to tell Scarpa that the home would have to be built on a tight budget. We told him we wanted a simple, Franciscan house, built with local materials and spacious."

Carlo Scarpa, not licensed as an architect because he had trained at the Academy of Fine Arts, had colleagues who could sign the project, including Sergio Los who took on the task and completed the work.

Five parallel non-rectilinear walls, following the course of the rows of vines on the ground, design the layout of the interiors and extend outward, giving each one a small private garden. Large windows create so many pictures of the vineyards and the vegetation that grows around

the building. Other windowed areas serve the interior by illuminating spaces, such as the kitchen, which have no outside views, and by allowing a continuous vision of the ceiling, the great protagonist of the interior. The size of these sheets of glass is such that they were installed during the construction work before the building was completed. The three levels on which the interior is laid out derive from the landforms, because not a single yard of land was excavated to build it.

The home is perceived by frames, by single shots without there being a main facade or rear. The valley side is mainly occupied by the living room, with the external side shaped with windows on the landscape and, on the inner side, the fireplace, the focus of the home. Placed on a higher level are the bedrooms that face uphill. Between the two, at an intermediate level, are the study and the service spaces.

During the summer, the happiest time of the year, the French windows occupying the head of the building are opened outward, letting the light, shade, and scents of blooms flood inside. The indoor flooring in split slabs of Val di Vizze stone, laid without grouting, continues outside, emphasizing that sense of continuity to which the design aspires. A series of terraced gardens are created between one wall and another, "outdoor rooms"—writes Gigliotti—or "*horti conclusi* that become extensions of the rooms in the home."

An element that imbues these spaces with poetry is the ceiling treated with lime, forming an origami-like pattern that draws diagonal lines, like a sheet of paper whose folds create real movement enriched by the color changes that run parallel to the walls. In the living room, the verticality of the space heightens the perception of its beauty and complexity.

CASA TABARELLI

The owners wanted the colors to change, from the sleeping area, where blue is paired with green, to the yellows and orange of the living room, following the movement of the sun from dawn to dusk. The internal walls with an irregular salmon-colored texture form a contrast due to the presence of bricks crumbled in the lime, while other walls, also treated with lime, remain white.

There are numerous details here: the industrial radiators set inside slits; the wooden bands surrounding the floors where the cables of the electrical system pass; the colored glass by Venini that embellishes the doors and windows. Never definitively completed, the lighting system is still entrusted to some bizarre-looking naked bulbs.

The surprises here are equally numerous: a sculpture by Scarpa on the mantelpiece, a Wassily white canvas armchair, of which Gavina was the first manufacturer, a fountain, with three others, by Andrea Branzi in the garden. And we cannot fail to mention the extraordinary sliding door that separates the living and sleeping areas, consisting of swivel tiles decorated with a geometric black-and-white design, different on the sides in order to create different patterns.

The feeling that Casa Tabarelli arouses in the visitor is that of a total project where every detail is eloquent, where the architecture blends with the lives of its clients, and where nature combines with works of art. There is no inside and outside, no spaces that the design imposes upon the inhabitants. On the contrary, the eye can lose itself in deep vistas, cross rooms that have different levels while joining in the intimacy of the kitchen—all designed, from the fireplace to the wooden log with its a designer repository, offering a cozy feel. The personality of Gianni and Laura Tabarelli has had a strong impact that remains unchanged, because the home has changed very little from its original state, including the furnishings that are mostly still those from the Gavina collection. The ownership has changed but, by a great stroke of luck, the villa has found a person sensitive to the beauty of the place in a contemporary art collector. Some tried to buy the home to modify and exploit its spaces. This would have been an unforgivable outrage. This is a home that needs to be safeguarded and defended from the passage of time, that has to be loved as it is, a timeless organism, a testament to a time that still lives on. It is not a museum home or an architectural work for insiders. It is right that its life, born from extraordinary synergy, should remain the same forever.

The entrance with a glimpse of the living room.

Following pages:
The large living room with original furnishings dating to the construction of the house, including the Marcel sofas from the 1960s by Kazuhide Takahama.

CASA TABARELLI

*Each room has a private green space with access through a French window and,
above, a glimpse of one of the French windows that closes the front of the building.
The stone floor continues outside and reaches the garden.*

Crescita by Carlo Scarpa and,
on the right, the development of the multicolored living room ceiling.
The dining area with a mobile sculpture by Bruno Munari is found where the vault dips.

Previous pages:
From the living room to the sleeping quarters there is a rise in elevation due to the landforms.
The sliding door introduces a decorative element of great impact.
Detail of the sliding door with movable mosaic tiles that change its geometry and,
to the right, a glimpse of the bedroom.

The studio located between the living room and the bedroom.

CASA TABARELLI

One of the cosiest rooms that has remained unchanged since the 1960s and,
above, detail of the colored glass inserts by Venini in the upper part of the windows.

Following pages, on the left:
The kitchen designed in every detail, from the fireplace to the large stump cutting board.
On the right: *Light enters from the large glazed areas offering glimpses of the colored ceiling.*
Detail of the development of the ceiling.

MUSEO CASA MOLLINO

MUSEO CASA MOLLINO
CARLO MOLLINO, TURIN, 1960–1968

The creation of a visionary, eclectic, and unconventional figure, the home that Carlo Mollino designed for himself without ever living in it is imbued with esoteric meaning. The merging of different eras, surrealist elements, and natural inspirations typical of his artistic language becomes a testament to the master architect from Turin.

t is with sincere regret that of all the interiors designed by Carlo Mollino, what remains today is only the home he made for himself, which he never lived in, on the banks of the Po River in Turin. It is magnificent, rich in mystery, the expression of a sophisticated, visionary, eclectic, and unconventional mind. And these qualities accentuate this regret for his other interior designs—no more than ten in all—of which only photographs remain, some taken by him.

Mollino was a true genius, a figure who thought outside the box, who left his mark on twentieth-century culture, and whose legacy still nurtures the contemporary imagination.

Born in 1905, his father was an engineer with a strong personality. Mollino graduated in architecture and developed exceptional competence in every field he devoted himself to. A solitary artist shrouded in mystery, he always lived in Turin. He found the city congenial, because it is "magical" and known as one of the three points in the triangle of white magic, the others being Prague and Lyon.

In elementary school, he designed the cross-sections of a car-engine cylinder and a camera. At the age of twenty-eight, he published a sort of autobiographical story, "The Life of Oberon," in *Casabella*, with the mythological king of the fairies as his double, capable of imagining a building and rotating it mentally with a technique that today is performed by computers. He could sketch with both hands and even draw two different designs on two separate sheets of paper, all at the same time. A race car driver, he designed a racing car. An experienced mountaineer and ski theorist, he wrote a manual, *Introduction to Downhill Skiing*, illustrating a new downhill technique. He was also an aerobatic pilot and a genius in mechanics and aerodynamics, fields in which he conducted numerous experiments. And above all he was a great architect, capable

Previous pages:
The living room with the fireplace designed by Mollino himself. The entryway with a shelf projecting from the large antique mirror and a Greek statue.

Detail of the wallpaper on photographic paper in the living room and the entryway seen through the sliding door by Campo e Graffi.

of exploring—in the ten buildings he designed—unique forms and solutions. The most famous of all, the last, is the Teatro Regio in Turin, completed shortly before his death in 1973, after seven years of work.

"The generation that he belonged to," wrote Paolo Portoghesi, an authority on Mollino's practice, "was that of Terragni, Gardella, Ridolfi, Albini, Scarpa, the architects who struggled to establish modern architecture in Italy with an independent identity. Among these architects, Mollino was the least rationalist, the most original and restless, the most influenced by literary culture . . . Twenty years ago it seemed that his unfortunate fate, as an architect *maudit*, risked erasing his extraordinary presence from Italy's architecture scene. Fortunately, changes of fashions and transformations of taste, together with the assiduous work of Fulvio and Napoleone Ferrari and Giovanni Brino, have restored him to the limelight."

It is thanks to Fulvio Ferrari that today we can visit his famous home at Via Napione 2 and draw on the lesson by which it not only introduces us to the history of that dwelling but, in light of his extensive research, offers a key to interpreting its esoteric meaning and above all explores the underlying enigma about why Mollino never lived there, despite the long years spent working on the project.

Fulvio Ferrari and his son Napoleone have done extensive research on the architect from Turin. Napoleone alone was responsible for the lastest, impressive volume *Carlo Mollino: Architect and Storyteller*, which analyzes his work as an architect.

The creation of a museum in the home dates to 1999, restored as faithfully as possible to its original state, after it had been turned into the office of an engineer (following Mollino's death) and the Italian State, in the absence of heirs, had sold off most of the furniture. Ferrari

then began to search for the original contents and recreate a world destined to disappear forever.

When Mollino rented the first floor inside the nineteenth-century Villa Avondo overlooking the river, he had three other apartments in Turin, not to mention that, despite owning these properties, he had lived for many years with his parents in a villa at Rivoli. He had a habit of renting apartments tailored to his needs. These included the famous Casa Miller, from 1936, one of his most sophisticated interior designs, used above all as a set for photographing in black and white his favorite female subjects.

The interiors of Via Napione 2, on which he worked from 1960 to 1968, were a sort of final summa of his ideas. There are surrealist elements, including horse heads and mirrors used with alienating effects (present in his initial projects), thus revealing how he was one of the first to understand this artistic movement.

Over the years, Mollino began to embrace an organicist vision, attracted by nature, its forms, and anthropomorphic shapes that influenced the design of his furnishings, which were often capable of reproducing the speed of a body in motion with limbs outstretched in leaps. In his home, nature is evoked in the seven black-and-white panels, more than 10 feet high, arranged in the living room at the sides of the fireplace, and in the opposite direction, in the dining room around the mirror, which recreate an engraving by Heinrich Böhmer (Düsseldorf, 1852–1930).

There are also his family heirlooms together with other objects, such as the Louis XV-style fireplace, which may look antique but which he actually designed himself. Intermingling eras and illusory games of time, memory, and eclecticism nurture the enigmatic and unique energy of this place.

By starting from his book on photography, *Il messaggio dalla camera oscura*, written by Mollino in 1943 and published in 1949, Ferrari believes he has found the end of a tangled skein. The title page of the book reproduces the Egyptian queen Tiye, an enigmatic sphinx, and by analyzing the dark chamber in Egyptian culture, represented by the heart of the pyramid where the soul of the deceased is housed in perpetuity, "the hypothesis emerges," writes Ferrari, "that in Via Napione the pharaoh-architect Mollino created a sort of *résidence d'éternité*." A home for the soul that has abandoned the body, a viaticum to face the journey that follows earthly existence.

There is no shortage of evocative details here: the oval mirror on the front door; the Vietri majolica floor that alludes to a garden with sliding Japanese-inspired doors; the two shells, symbols of eternity, which flank the French window in the central area; the number of chairs—eight—in the dining room; the table consisting of an oval top resting on two columns (of Hercules?). And the bedroom, the second of two where Mollino never slept even for a single night, confirms these suppositions thanks to the boat bed—necessary for the journey—on the blue carpet reminiscent of a river, the animalier upholstery—a memory of the high priest dressed in leopard skin who presides over the rites in the tomb of the pharaoh—and the 316 butterflies brought together in sixty-four panels—a symbol of rebirth. All clues that support Ferrari's thesis.

True or not, the hypothesis of Mollino as an occultist adds interest to his figure as an architect, the creator of original interiors, a designer who never worked for any manufacturer, the author of unique pieces that today are auctioned at incredible prices.

Obsessed with forms, he aspired to a kind of naturalism that in him could only be cerebral and abstract, viewing nature as his sole guide.

"The home where the warrior rests," as Mollino himself described it, conjures a strong symbolic image for the visitor, who does not escape unscathed from such an engaging immersion.

In the year of his death, the architect wrote to a friend: "As the Chinese of high rank adorns his mausoleum in life, so I am preparing, in my late maturity, in a corridor in my house, a kind of sunset boulevard with a sequence of photographs and memories of my life: all, or almost all, are very beautiful."

Previous pages:
The interior seen through the mirror-finish porthole of the front door. The two valves of the giant clam (Tridacna gigas) *in front of the French window overlooking the river.*

Detail of the Japanese lamp in the living room and,
on the right, the fireplace and wallpaper on photographic paper.

Previous pages:
The theatrical atmosphere in the living room with curtains, capitonné chairs, and a plaster-cast horse head.

In the dining room, Tulip chairs by Eero Saarinen, table by Carlo Mollino, and a Japanese lamp.
On the floor, the model of a car designed by the architect from Turin.

Previous pages:
Vietri tiles in the bathroom and on the floor of the entryway.

The bedroom with the boat bed and the animalier pattern on the walls.
Above, 316 butterflies arranged on 64 panels.

CASA
MENDINI

CASA MENDINI

ALESSANDRO MENDINI,
OLDA VAL TALEGGIO, 2006

In the *buen retiro* the architect
Alessandro Mendini created for
himself and his family, everything
speaks of him, of his aesthetic,
of his research into the memory
of places and things, providing
a stage for his boundless
imagination: colors cover the walls
and overspread the furnishings,
the carpets are reminiscent of his
drawings, and the objects are those
designed over a lifetime.

Previous pages:
Mendini's studio with the Cipriani mirror-fronted cocktail cabinet, the Amuleto lamp on a table by Anna Gili, and the large B vase.
On the Proust II carpet, by Sotiros Papadopulos, the Ondoso table.

Two views of the exterior.

"I've always rejected the idea of designing a house for myself. I've had some more or less beautiful homes in my life, but I deliberately kept them away from that precise idea that, for an architect, is called 'deciding the design of your own domestic space.'"

This is what Alessandro Mendini wrote about his vacation home at Olda, in the Bergamo valleys, which, against the grain of his own ideas, led him "albeit belatedly and finally" to identify with the design of a living space that represents him, "a domestic place 'where I feel at home,' decorated for myself (and in any case, I thought ahead: for only a few days a year, it's a holiday home!)."

In the French-inspired art nouveau villa, nestled in a mountainous landscape some 3,000 feet above sea level, not far from the Grand Hotel of San Pellegrino Terme (also dating to the early twentieth century), Mendini, for short periods starting in 2006, found his *buen retiro* with his daughters Fulvia and Elisa and his grandchildren.

Architect, artist, writer, and a prominent figure in publishing as the editor of numerous magazines, a radical designer and designer for industry, Alessandro Mendini, born in 1931, was a theorist and intellectual who conditioned the renewal of twentieth-century design culture.

Gio Ponti, a sort of putative father, passed the baton on to him by inviting him to direct *Domus* in 1979. This prestigious role followed his previous editorship, from 1970 to 1975, of *Casabella*, which Mendini turned into an authoritative mouthpiece for Radical Design, providing the magazines, as Fulvio Irace wrote in his publication *Codice Mendini*, with "accelerated growth, building a network of relationships and opinions that managed to capture the best creative energies on the international scene, opening doors and windows to the Italian debate on the most disparate worlds." He is also credited with founding the magazine *Modo*, where he acted as director from 1977 to 1981.

In 1976, on the initiative of Alessandro and Adriana Guerriero, the Alchimia design firm was founded. Mendini was asked to join in 1978, together with Ettore Sottsass, Andrea Branzi, and Michele De Lucchi, and his collaboration with it continued until 1987. Work teams, seminars, debates, and products, full- and part-time collaborators elaborated the themes of deconstruction, alternative design, and postmodernity. But it would be, above all, the decorative experiments conducted by Mendini with Alchimia that would win the Compasso d'Oro in 1981.

Graphic patterns, complex decorations, lettering, and doodles visually embodying his thoughts are the stylistic hallmark of Mendini's universe, garnering enormous success with his iconic Poltrona di Proust armchair. In 1978, the author swathed an eighteenth-century-inspired armchair in the signs and colors of the post-impressionist painter Signac: not just the upholstery, but also the wooden volutes of its frame are covered with a pointillist decoration. It became an icon, the "royal ancestor of the lineage of redesign" as Irace called it, and a manifesto of postmodernism. A limited-edition piece, it would also be made in bronze and ceramic and, later, covered with glass mosaic tiles for Bisazza.

During his lifetime, Alessandro Mendini wrote extensively. Some titles of his books, speeches, and editorials suggest some lines of thought: "Architecture Farewell, Unhappy Project," "Ollo. Magazine without a Message," "Trivial House," "Objects for Spiritual Use," and "Subtle Survival" all evoke a philosophy that has questioned design, "the grayness of functionality," "the anonymity of the series," in favor of emotional qualities and the transience of things and thoughts. And they reveal fragments of his

persona, which, under the passion for color, decoration, and irony, conceal a solitary and nostalgic vein, aware that utopia is an extraordinary driving force, "the mythical model toward which to strive. It is important that it should be unattainable."

For Mendini, man—understood as body, psyche, and spirit—was central, and spaces were the psychological representation of those who lived in them. Throughout his career, he put himself on the line, with numerous self-portraits, as a Harlequin or with a halo, recounting in person—with light, profound prose—his experiences as an inhabitant, creator, explorer of the origins of things, and promoter of reuse, crafts, and manual workmanship. A vocation already expressed in his last name: Mendini, which derives from *ram-mendini* [also in English, *to mend*]. It is the name of a humble medieval craft, the person who adjusts, stitches, and makes new by assembling old parts.

His villa at Olda—with its rich past, when it was originally built as a private residence and then a summer vacation home for disabled children—is the expression of his research into the feelings of places, memories, and family heritage.

"In approaching the restoration, the new criteria of use, and the new habits and customs together with Fulvia and Elisa," he wrote, "I thought of designing a 'figurative' genre of furniture. In fact, I wanted to create a place that would express the figures of our lives. Their documentation through a complex system of furnishings and references, reflections of each other. I wanted to make a home to experience in a mental as well as real way, where spaces, colors, furniture, and objects describe the iconography of our lives, passions, and interests . . . It is the staging of an elaborate vacuum to contain the story of my life." It is, in fact, the objects that Mendini designed over a long span of time that inhabit the home, not as in a museum or in some celebratory sense, but "as if my works were a request for a sense of welcome, protection, intimacy, and abandonment."

"The Things We Are" is the beautiful title Mendini gave to the installation of the third edition of the Triennale di Milano Design Museum in 2010.

And here in Olda, the objects speak about him. At the entrance, the large Montesquieu resin vase welcomes you. It is part of a series of exercises that Mendini conducted on the scale of objects, on their dimensions, and on how subjective their perception is. "Unbalancing gymnastics," as he called them, and by proposing the theme of the "Gulliver effect" he asks a fundamental question: "When, at what moment, is a dimension right or wrong?"

The idea behind many of his designs is tangible at Olda: transforming the ordinary into the extraordinary and making the home a stage for his dreams and memories. This vision includes numerous colorful carpets that seem to make his designs walkable. The exercise of filling pages and pages with signs, diagrams, graphics, and chromatic research never left him, and his visual alphabet was close to the world of art, with which he collaborated in a mutual exchange between disciplines. After all, in the 2006 drawing titled *I am not an architect I am a dragon*, Mendini pictured himself as a strange creature with the body of an architect, the head of a designer, the hands of a craftsman, the chest of a manager, the belly of a priest, the feet of an artist, the legs of a graphic designer, and the tail of a poet.

At Olda, colors cover the walls—green, lilac, lobster red—which act as a counterpoint to the patterns of the original floors in decorated tiles. And then different shades on all the furnishings, many of which are painted with small dots, the same that made his Proust armchair famous and then became a leitmotif in his paintings, accessories, and carpets. "They are romantic, like a cloud of motes, and they make objects lose their edges."

The domestic scale of Olda does not contradict the significant architecture designed by Atelier Mendini—the Groninger Museum in Holland, the Alessi factories, the Materdei station on the Naples subway line—nor the numerous objects on which he collaborated with the finest design companies. Nor does it diminsh the figure of the master awarded the Ordre des Arts et des Lettres and the accolades of the Architectural League of New York. Instead, it enables us to discover, behind the facade of a villa that seems straight out of a fairy tale, his most private and emotional world and to read with empathy Fulvio Irace's description of it: "Seen as a whole, the furnishings and architecture, drawings, decorations, and words of Mendini exude this type of *Sehnsucht* (difficulty) that literary criticism has historically attributed to Romantic sensibility: an unfulfilled desire, combined with the aspiration to become one with nature and with the perceptual and existential world, rather than the political or social one. A melancholy gaze that projects onto reality a crepuscular and autobiographical vision that nurtures a personal, silent worship of memory."

The entryway with the Montesquieu vase. The briarwood furniture comes from the period furnishings of the Grand Hotel in San Pellegrino Terme.

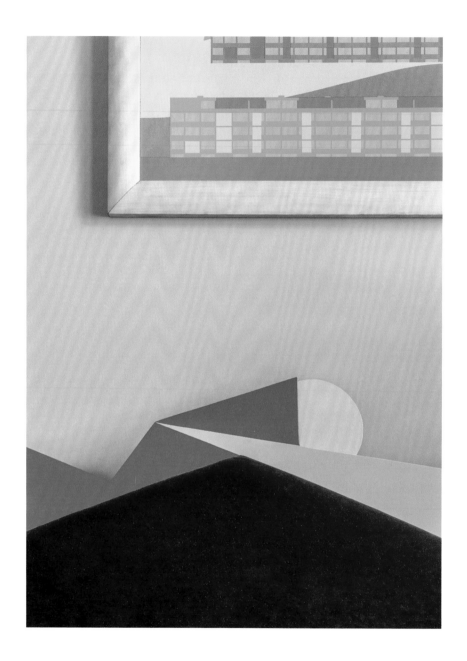

Detail of the Kandissi sofa and,
on the right, the same sofa surmounted by a Weissenhof painting.
On the floor, the Ollo carpet and, under the window, nineteenth-century chairs upholstered
with Proust fabric.

*In the bedroom, the furnishings and accessories are all by Alessandro Mendini: the Quo storage unit,
the Christina carpet, the Mandala painting, the bed and bedside tables with Galla Placidia pictorial redesign.*

Following pages:
*In the grandchildren's gameroom everything is expressed in Mendini's language, from the dresser
with pictorial redesign to the famous Poltrona di Proust armchair and Cornucopia carpet.*

*Glimpse of the living room with the Pulviscolo painting, the Aliot lamp,
the Murillo sofa, the Veneziano cabinet, and the Superego column.*

Detail of the Senza Titolo *painting and the* Colonnina *with the* Fontanina *sculpture.*

Following pages:
Glimpse of the bedroom with the Proust *bed and detail of the headboard.*

The studio with a Poltrona di Proust armchair, Mendinismi vases, and Senza Titolo carpet.
Above, two glimpses of the landing with the Ameba carpet and two Sedile chairs from the
Museo Bagatti Valsecchi.

On the terrace, a Poltrona di Proust in the outdoor version and,
on the right, the garden of the villa with the Proust table in Bisazza mosaic.

CASA CRESPI

CASA CRESPI

GABRIELLA CRESPI, MILAN, SINCE 1970

This home in Milan represents the creative and life journey of a trailblazing designer. It is replete with limited editions and unique pieces, self-made and with great attention to detail; furniture transformed by complex invisible mechanisms; and lamps and sculptures inspired by the animal kingdom. It possesses the wayward personality of a free and independent spirit on an incessant quest for a language all her own.

Amythical aura surrounds her. Her beauty is eloquent in the portraits that renowned photographers took of her. The furniture she designed fetches substantial sums at international auctions. Gabriella Crespi, a creator of furniture and accessories, was an eccentric figure on the Italian scene and in Milan during the 1970s, when celebrated architect designers had already established the uniqueness of Italian design and taken it beyond national borders.

She remained outside all this, isolated and aloof, known to international jet-setters, who were her public and included the most famous celebrities.

At the time, serial production reigned supreme and celebrated its culture, encompassing all fields of production, from cars to household appliances and furniture. It was even the topic of critical analysis at MoMA in New York with the exhibition curated by Emilio Ambasz, *Italy: The New Domestic Landscape*.

At the same time, Gabriella Crespi followed her own path and stood out by creating objects that had the allure of limited editions, lavishing great care on the details and the expression of fine craftsmanship.

She was born in 1922, into an artistic family thanks to her mother, Emma Caimi Pellini, who made costume jewelry for haute-couture maisons that, in the 1950s, was displayed in the windows of Saks Fifth Avenue, New York, and won second and third place at the *Imitation of the Jewel* exhibition at the Milan Triennale in 1950.

Gabriella Pellini Crespi's decision to attend the School of Architecture, enrolling in 1944, was trailblazing. Women in the field were rare at the time: Franca Helg, Anna Castelli Ferrieri, Cini Boeri, and Gae Aulenti were among the first to break the taboo of architecture as a male discipline, struggling with great determination to affirm their identity as professionals. Crespi did not graduate, but she resonated with the intellectual stimuli suggested by the ideas of Le Corbusier and Frank Lloyd Wright.

Her home in Milan, now the premises of the Gabriella Crespi Archive, makes it possible to retrace an entire career that began with small precious accessories and then developed into major collections, including the most iconic objects, tables that embody complex mechanisms, lamps, and sculptures.

Her achievement is difficult to classify. It does not follow a linear path or a progression of themes, with the most recent replacing earlier ones. On the contrary, figuration and abstraction alternate, decoration and geometry are expressed simultaneously, surrealist promptings and formal purity all coexist. Her creativity was explosive, as revealed today by her daughter Elisabetta, her first assistant and her irreplaceable right-hand woman.

In 1948 her marriage to Giuseppe Maria Crespi, a member of the family of textile industrialists and co-owners of the *Corriere della Sera*, whose children were Elisabetta and Gherardo, strengthened her circle, which included the nobility and the Milanese upper middle class. Her first works were made for her enjoyment and from a creative drive, with the goal of offering friends and acquaintances objects crafted by her own hands; she used antique materials mounted on forms to create original paperweights or card holders. This then led to increasingly sophisticated collections, thus revealing her courageous entrepreneurial vision and ability to establish herself as a brand capable of achieving international fame. Among her first iconic objects, the Lune lamp in nickel-plated and gilt brass, attracted the attention of Maison Dior, which perceived in its soft and sculptural form the stylized design of the letters "CD." This was the start of a decade-long collaboration with the Parisian fashion house, for which Crespi designed table accessories, jewelry, and even furniture. Years later, in around 2008, another designer, Stella McCartney, was attracted by the same lamp, glimpsing the "S" of her name in it. Captivated by Crespi's charisma, she asked her to make a small series of limited-edition jewelry in bronze and semiprecious stones, with proceeds being donated to an Indian hospital.

In 1964, Crespi moved to Rome and opened her home-showroom in the ancient Palazzo Cenci. Being invited to the presentation of its collections, which inaugurated every six months, was a privilege. Rome's *beau monde* and business people came together there. One could encounter Audrey Hepburn accompanied by Hubert de Givenchy or Shams Pahlavi, sister of the Shah of Persia, making purchases on behalf of her brother. She also opened shops in Milan, first on Via Borgospesso and then Via Montenapoleone, where they were frequented by the Thyssen family, Gunter Sachs, and Paola of Liège, among others.

In Gabriella Crespi's final home, the middle of the large living room hosts the Ellisse table, from the Plurimi series, displayed in 2016 at the Triennale di Milano in the exhibition *W. Women in Italian Design*. Designed in 1976, it supports the sculpture *My Soul*, into which Crespi infused much of herself and her personality.

The Plurimi, covering a long span of time from 1970 to 1982, is comprised of numerous pieces representing the central body of Crespi's practice: substantial volumes, beveled forms made even brighter and softer by brass, with planes that extend and retract moved by secret mechanisms. Metamorphic pieces thanks to their transformative abilities, Plurimi pays tribute to the artist Emilio Vedova.

Throughout her career, Crespi always had close ties with the art world. A great friend of the art critic and publisher Vanni Scheiwiller, who greatly praised her work, as

The sculpture Cervo in inlaid Lebanese cedar and,
above, the Fungo lamp on the Hi-Fi table.
In the background, the bar cabinet-bookcase from the Menhir series.

well as the French architect Jacques Couëlle, the Milanese designer engaged in imaginative dialogues with Salvador Dalí, Diego Giacometti, François-Xavier, and Claude Lalanne. With Lalanne she shared a love for the animal kingdom, explored through a poetic and surreal lens. Over the years, Crespi created a very personal bestiary with allusions to the world of fairy tales, expressed with a highly realistic and precise formal language in detail. Rhinos and herons, tortoises and hippos, ostriches and deer of different sizes were made in bronze using the ancient lost-wax method and in wood inlaid by hand. Inside, many of them have a blown-glass egg, the result of her historic collaboration with the masters of the Barovier&Toso glassworks.

The entryway of her home leads to the dining room, where seventeenth-century furnishings from Palazzo Cenci contain silver objects intended to decorate the table with Renaissance richness, with the great table of the *Rising Sun* series dominating the entire space. It was a new chapter in the artist's journey when she began to apply bamboo to furniture, lamps, and even a cradle, revealing her skill in working with different materials—be they metals, stone, or the most modest and flexible natural fibers. Here as in her other creations, the relationship with nature plays a central part, not only as the only great source of inspiration but as a sign of her profound connection with the universe. An intense spirituality distinguished her and intimately marked her personality since childhood. Beyond the fashionable and wealthy she mingled with, she was a restless and profound soul, in search of her own mystical path, which she explored with great suffering. When she turned sixty-five in

1987, it was the end of an era. She left everything behind and traveled to India, living there for twenty years and finding her long-sought-after spiritual guide in the master Shri Muniraji.

On returning to Milan for a brief visit, an accident forced her to stay there, but without ceasing her inner search, meditative practices, and contact with her teacher. She wrote the book *Search for Infinity. Himalaya*, and assisted by Elisabetta, she returned to her former profession by reissuing some of her most beloved pieces in new materials. Six years before her death in 2017, she finally received official recognition from Milan's cultural world with the exhibition *Gabriella Crespi. The Sign and the Spirit* at Palazzo Reale in Milan.

Crespi was above all an artist, applying her talent to creating practical objects, some of which are very functional. Yet she always fostered her uniqueness and, not just professionally but also humanly, explored a path that was hers alone. A traveler (among the first women to enter China in the 1970s), a lover of archeology, and an author of verses, Crespi was a pioneer of a very current trend—intertwining different periods and promoting cultured eclecticism (for example, the frescoes in Palazzo Cenci acting as a backdrop to her streamlined furniture). Today we talk of Collectible Design, a reality that responds to the need to avoid serial production and to nurture the tradition of fine craftsmanship. Gabriella Crespi heralded all this and defended her independence with self-production—without falling for the blandishments of the industry—while pursuing her own freedom.

The Cervo magnifying glass on the folding table.

Detail of the prototype of the Rising Sun table and,
above, a view of the dining area.
The pair of candlesticks belongs to the Gocce Oro collection.

On the desk, Gabriella's notes and her book, Search for Infinity. Himalaya.
On the right, the Fungo lamp.

A portrait of Gabriella Crespi in the 1960s and the lamp-sculpture Lune.
Above, on the table, the lamp Conchiglia, Ippopotamo con piccolo, and,
in the center, Piccole Lune.

CASA
FORNASE

CASA FORNASETTI

PIERO AND BARNABA FORNASETTI,
MILAN, SINCE 1950

A minimal Milanese building conceals a surprising *Wunderkammer*, bearing exceptional testimony to the Fornasetti family's fantastical universe. The furniture, decorations, tiles, wallpapers, drawings, objects—everything revolves around the creative parabola that began with Piero and continues, constantly renewed, with his son Barnaba.

Previous pages:
*In the green living room with
Chesterfield sofas, a pair of lamps, and,
among the bookcases, the mirrored City
cabinet.
In the music room, tray
by Piero Fornasetti and tools.*

Two views of the garden.

n Milan, on a rather ordinary street in the Città Studi district, behind a nondescript facade, a garden which was once an old vegetable patch leads to the enchanted world of Barnaba Fornasetti. Fantasy, eccentricity, and imagination are some of the extraordinary ingredients that marked the path of his father Piero—artist, poet, printer, graphic designer, decorator, and collector; Barnaba, with great intelligence, has succeeded in safeguarding this legacy.

Piero Fornasetti was born in 1913 into a wealthy bourgeois family and lived in this same home built by his father in the late nineteenth century on what were then the outskirts of Milan. Piero devoted himself to numerous disciplines: he was a great draftsman, painter, and printer of works by other artists, including De Chirico, and he created his own artistic language that made him, from early on, decidedly unmistakable on the international scene. Figurative subjects gave rise to splendid colorful porcelains, oils on panel, watercolors on paper, temperas, and pastels on which he built his fruitful career as a decorator, without ever forgetting that the origin of his practice was pictorial and his fortune lay "in being born a painter, and as a painter working with the most intense imagination." His knowledge of printing and engraving techniques was the result of constant experimentation. People imagined that he knew some secret techniques and he laughed about this, saying: "My only secret is the rigor with which I conduct my work, the serenity of my choices, and I hope that in time my critical sense will not decline."

At the age of twenty he made his mark at the Milan Triennale with a series of printed silk scarves. Gio Ponti took notice, calling them "graphic sonnets," and from then on became his supporter and great admirer. But their relationship never went beyond formal terms over the course of a long collaboration that gave rise to the frescoes in Palazzo del Bo, the campus at the University of Padua, numerous interiors and furnishings, home decorations, ship cabins, and even cinemas. The director of Domus went so far as to declare: "If one day the story of my life is written, a chapter should be titled *Passion for Fornasetti*."

Together with his work as a painter and printer, Fornasetti always compulsively collected other people's motifs, taking them from popular culture, erudite quotations, zoology, and botany to create an immense archive on which he would draw to decorate any object, furnishing, or artifact. Obelisks and playing cards, hands of all forms, butterflies, snakes, entire libraries of open and closed books, imaginary cities, the pages of newspapers, Suns and clouds, gardens and archaeological finds, architectural themes and musical instruments. The list could go on indefinitely because there was no iconographic theme that Fornasetti's imagination did not elaborate. And there is no furnishing or accessory that has not been "tattooed" in the manner of Fornasetti.

The house where Barnaba grew up was, and still is, the place where most of his creations were devised, in a wing built later to complete the main building. Home and workshop formed a single whole, and still do, because during Piero's time one moved between the offices and exhibition spaces where the client could choose, while today—since the Atelier Fornasetti boasts a splendid shop on three floors in the center of Milan—Barnaba loves to open his home for events dedicated not only to his work but also to theater, literature, and music, for which he has a great passion.

The method of Piero, the creative genius, who expressed a fantastical world without limits, with references spanning from ancient Rome to the Renaissance and surrealism, corresponded to his great scrupulousness in the production of furniture and objects and his systematic accuracy in managing his immense archive, where everything was catalogued with maniacal precision. In an article devoted to him by M, the magazine of *Le Monde*, Barnaba recounted his childhood: "I was born at the same time as the Atelier. We grew up together. I was raised among artisans, amid the smell of damp paper and colors. I was aware of the arguments and remember my father, standing in the middle of the room, speaking into a sort of megaphone. My mother, his great accomplice, constantly reminded me how she and my father worked day and night and that I, an idle youngster, should follow their example. I grew up in an atmosphere of permanent productive creativity. Everything in the house revolved around work and ideas taking shape. I watched, listened in silence, and climbed up the craftsmen's legs to ask them to help me repaint my toy cars. 'Inspiration lies everywhere,' my father repeated, and this was the first lesson I remember in my education."

In the Atelier on the ground floor, work instruments, tools of the trade, jars of paint, and prototypes to develop are all lined up. In the entryway, however, a display case on the wall contains small objects from the immense catalogue that in the golden years totaled 13,000, when Piero opened a large showroom on Via Montenapoleone. Barnaba loves to tend to it by often creating new displays.

Over time, the rooms in the home have changed function, but the spirit of total and immersive design, typical of the Fornasetti universe, remains. Collecting is part of it: on the green living room wall, with the collection of mirrors that combine ancient *sorcières* with creations by Piero and Barnaba, and in the magnificent Biedermeier tumblers placed with great effect in front of a window.

The room that has changed least over time is probably the master bedroom, painted whale blue. Together

In the kitchen, the furnishings and floor tiles are decorated with the Ultime Notizie pattern.
The large painting, The Butterfly Seller, *is by Piero. On the table, ceramic by Fausto Salvi.*

with the large nineteenth-century gilt iron bed, it displays typical pieces produced in the 1950s: the four-drawer desk made for the interiors of the Casa Ceccato in Milan, the result of a collaboration with Ponti, who created the design, and a pair of curved dressers decorated respectively with masonry interspersed with small black windows and a drawing inspired by Palladian architecture, though it is actually a sixteenth-century Austrian villa.

The dresser is a traditional type in its lines, a rigorous form with a convexity that assists the application of the design. It represents the ideal in Piero's philosophy, which aspires to simple and severe forms that set off the patterns.

The curved dresser was created for the vacation home in Varenna, where the family spent long periods and from which many furnishings present here derive. The room immersed in red comes from that villa, a nightmare that puts you in a good mood, a game taken to the extreme since the library contains only books that have the word "red" in the title.

The kitchen, by contrast, is bright and poetic, filled with sunlight and overlooking the garden. Here the theme is that of butterflies, perching on the latest articles in the newspapers about Fornasetti and covering the furniture and floor with an all-over pattern, together with the complicit gaze of *The Butterfly Seller* painted by Piero in 1938.

Over time, the greatness of Fornasetti was recognized more abroad than at home. It was a Frenchman, Patrick Mauriès, who in 1987 dedicated a book to him that Piero regrettably never lived to see published. In 1983, the trumeau Architettura, an iconic piece of the Atelier, was auctioned by Christie's in New York for the record sum of $15,000. Previously, the opening in London of the Themes & Variations gallery had rekindled interest after a less successful period. It was in 1982 that Barnaba returned to Milan, prompted by his father who needed his help to emerge from a period of difficulties regarding their identity and finances. Since then, the son has become more Fornasettian than the father. He has restored the Atelier to its former glory, identifying a suitable market segment, reissuing the most famous pieces, creating new ones, and establishing a series of collaborations with companies producing upholstery, fabrics, and carpets. Barnaba has also installed numerous exhibitions, published his father's complete works in two huge volumes for Electa, produced an opera by Mozart, and much more.

With the home generously open to cultural and musical events, Piero's aura continues to emanate all its charm, and from the archive, holding over 13,000 drawings, come ideas, inventions, and fantastical objects that are also definitely useful. "Now we all say," stated Piero, "the modern was stillborn, the rational is futile, and salvation lies in form. What harebrained ideas! Salvation lies in the imagination."

The Gerusalemme wallpaper created specifically for this wall. In the background, a painting by Valeria Manzi and a vintage screen decorated with the Foulards print. The head on the chest of drawers is a sculpture Piero made when he was a youth.

In the studio, archive drawers, samples, prototypes, and exhibition posters.

Following pages:
On the yellow walls of the entryway, a display case as a Wunderkammer,
a sequence of calendar plates, and furniture with the Libri *print.*

Previous pages, on the left: *Detail of the library.*
On the right: *The Riga desk and Squadra by Barnaba Fornasetti and the Battaglia Navale screen.*

On the wall of the green living room, an antique mirror and a collection of cameos and,
above, a collection of Biedermeier glasses.

Following pages:
*Piero and Giulia's bedroom covered with Nuvole wallpaper. In one corner, a desk by Gio Ponti
decorated with the Biglietti da visita print. Facing the bed is a vintage curved chest
of drawers with the Palladiana design.*

A total look for the bathroom, covered with the Tema e Variazioni print.

Following pages:
The red room reserved for guests; on the walls, the Chiavi segrete wallpaper.
An anthology of the Fornasetti family's decorative flair.

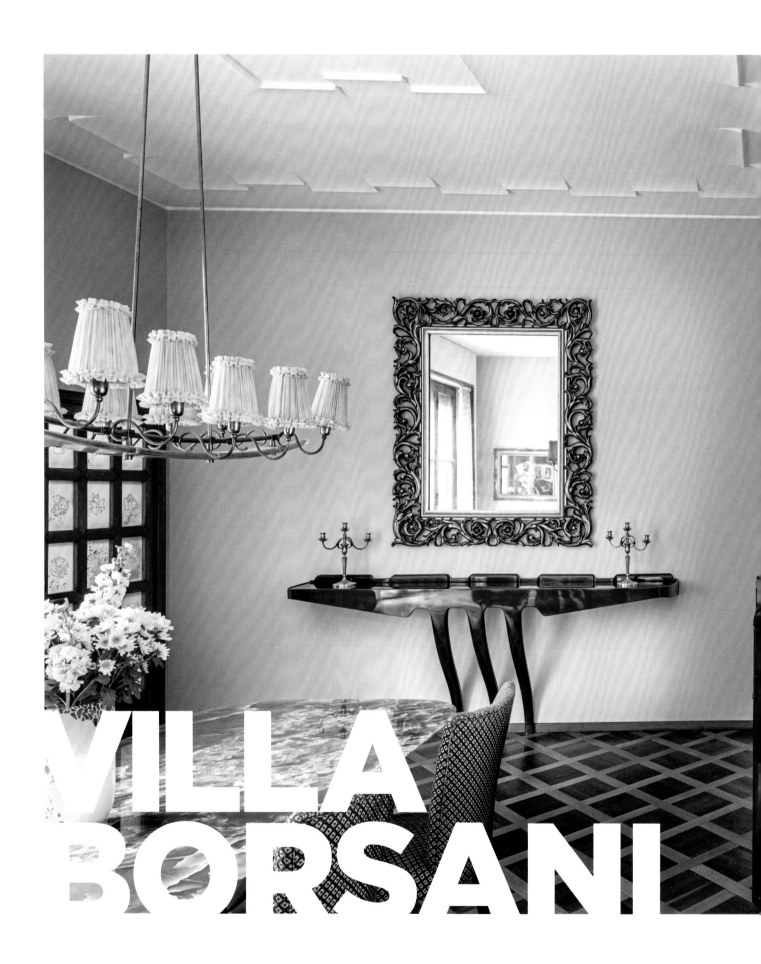

VILLA BORSANI

VILLA BORSANI
OSVALDO BORSANI, VAREDO, 1943–1945

Osvaldo Borsani designed this masterpiece—a union of architecture, interiors, and furnishings. Here he expressed the artistic and entrepreneurial trajectory of a Lombard family that successfully took design from the workshop to serial production.

Previous pages:
The dining room with a glimpse
of the entryway.
A detail of the card table by the artist
Piccardo.

The streamlined facade
and the entrance porch.

The villa that Osvaldo Borsani designed and built between 1943 and 1945 for his parents, and where he lived with them, his twin brother Fulgenzio, and their families, is located at Varedo, some twelve miles from Milan. A major figure in Italian product design, uniquely distinguished in the threefold role of architect, designer, and entrepreneur, Borsani built the villa on land adjoining the factory founded by his father Gaetano: ABV, Arredamenti Borsani Varedo. Osvaldo had just turned thirty and had already accumulated a series of successes after his studies, first at the Brera Academy and then at the School of Architecture in Milan, where he graduated in 1937.

In 1933, while still a student, he won the silver medal at the 5th Triennale with his design for the Casa Minima, the prototype for limited-space housing.

The villa in Varedo, which now hosts the archive of his numerous designs as well as those of his heirs, who carried on the family business after him, is considered a masterpiece of integration between architecture, interiors, and furnishings. It is interesting both architecturally and by the emblematic history it embodies: that of a family of entrepreneurs who combined craft skills with technology, invention, and respect for tradition and who contributed decisively to spreading Italian manufacturing worldwide.

It all began with his grandfather Paolo, who made furniture by hand, followed by Gaetano, with the creation of Atelier Borsani in 1923, which later became ABV in 1933. Then in 1953 Tecno was established by Osvaldo and Fulgenzio. Valeria, Osvaldo's daughter, her husband Marco Fantoni, and Paolo, Fulgenzio's son, played a pivotal role in developing the family brand; Tommaso Fantoni, an architect like his parents, is now responsible for the archive and ABV—still active regarding the historic products—together with Federico, Paolo's son.

The family of designers revolved around Osvaldo, a charismatic figure, not only in the family setting; he was outstanding on the Italian and international scene for the creation of timeless furnishings and prestigious interiors in the evolution of home living. The major exhibition devoted to Osvaldo's oeuvre by the Triennale di Milano in 2018 testified to this. The exhibit design was by Norman Foster and Tommaso Fantoni, coinciding with the publication of a richly documented monumental volume edited by Giampiero Bosoni.

Here the historian and theorist Daniel Sherer drew a parallel between the villa in Varedo and two masterpieces of twentieth-century fiction, Thomas Mann's *Buddenbrooks* and Robert Musil's *The Man without Qualities*, seeing the house as their architectural equivalent. "In his hands," Sherer wrote, "architecture became a powerful cultural metaphor for the creation of an epos that thematized the expanded narrative of his family."

A detached, independent building set in a large garden, the villa has a very minimal exterior made up of austere volumes arranged asymmetrically. This is the result of a rationalist idea to which Borsani adhered, tempered by a professional practice in which he created a bridge between modernity and classicism. A portico with a pergola acts as a filter and leads to the entryway, which has perhaps the most spectacular feature of the entire design: the magnificent staircase connecting the two floors of the building, which over time has become an iconic image of twentieth-century architecture. Made of Candoglia marble quarried in Val d'Ossola (the same material that was used to build Milan's cathedral), it has handrails in solid walnut, brass detailing, and a parapet consisting of tempered glass strips with tapering forms. The background is a large window that offers a view of the two flights of steps as they

cross, making them look even lighter and more buoyantly suspended. The design of the two-tone floor is also important, with a decorative wave pattern alluding to the imagery of the Sienese landscape.

On the ground floor of the building there is a large living room overlooking the garden and the dining room, set on a slightly higher level resting on a base of green Alpi marble. In this respect, architectural historians stress the influence of the Viennese architect Adolf Loos and his ideas in relation to domestic interiors, conceived not as uniform spaces but characterized by staggered levels. In Villa Borsani, the raised dining room creates a vista through the living room toward the garden. From here, it is said, Gaetano Borsani loved to keep an eye on both the factory and the entrance to his villa.

Lombard industriousness and genius are evoked by these interiors, more luxurious and decorated—with hints of art deco—than the exterior suggests. The furnishings of the home, from the original ones to those designed later, represent an anthology of ABV and Tecno production and are exemplary of the centrality of craftsmanship and subsequently the results achieved in high-end industrial production. This is because Borsani's professional career spans the whole evolution of the twentieth century and its memorable phases, representing the taste of the Milanese bourgeoisie with great elegance and then producing furniture with Tecno that anticipated the future. For example, Graphis, the first flexible office system, which made the company a world leader, or Modus, the first nylon shell ever printed. Not to mention the D70 sofa, the P40 armchair, and the AT16 coat hanger, which have become icons of Borsani's creativity.

As Giampiero Bosoni wrote: "Borsani interpreted in an independent and original way one of the most

The elegant staircase, and, above, a detail of the parapet.

Following pages:
*The central living room with D120 sofas by Valeria Borsani and Alfredo Bonetti
and a chandelier by Guglielmo Ulrich.*

significant developments in the history of Italian design celebrated worldwide. From craftsmanship to industry, from charcoal or watercolor drawing to the birth of digital design, from the work of the cabinetmaker to mechanical serial production, from the refined contribution of artists to state-of-the-art care of the technical detailing . . . from the local market to international markets."

What the villa embodies with extreme originality provides a crucial clue to understanding Osvaldo Borsani's achievement, namely the relationship between the entrepreneur, architect, and designer with the artists of his generation. His time at Brera Academy was essential in forging relationships that lasted and gave rise to numerous collaborations. Many of them took the form of interior design projects of which, unfortunately, photographs provide the only remaining trace. On the other hand, Osvaldo had already developed a remarkable sensibility for the artistic milieu in his father's workshop, where the furniture had often been enriched by the work of artists since the 1930s. Milan in the 1950s witnessed great cultural fervor, dominated by an interdisciplinary outlook in which architecture, furniture, and art experimented with a new vocabulary and engaged in a dialogue that mutually nurtured their different fields. This included their relationship with Lucio Fontana. The designer of the magnificent ceramic fireplace in the villa's large living room and the small polychrome ceramic depicting a Madonna and Child placed outside, the Italian-Argentinian artist has left his mark in numerous furnishings and interiors created by Borsani. Environmental works, with the creation of wall or ceiling decorations with baroque volutes and polychrome stucco, are flanked, in shared projects, by furnishings in which the artist added

decorations that brought a significant aesthetic enhancement to the functionality of the piece. Passersby who glance up at the facade of Via Montenapoleone 27 in Milan make a precious discovery: the iron balustrade of the long balcony designed by Fontana. And it is here that Tecno opened its showroom in 1955 just two years after its foundation.

The culture of dialogue was something Borsani nurtured with numerous artists, whose works are present in the villa. Next to the staircase is an iron sculpture by Agenore Fabbri, who also left his mark on some of the furnishings. Arnaldo Pomodoro created the sculptural headboards (including one on the first floor) and contributed to an ambitious residential design on the Caspian Sea. Adriano Spilimbergo, a former collaborator of his father Gaetano, designed the floral mosaic decorating the master bathroom. Alongside these names, Luca Crippa, Aligi Sassu, and Fausto Melotti should also be remembered. The villa bears witness to significant encounters between its owners and the Milanese cultural milieu, with an international gaze on the world of design, despite the fact that Borsani is remembered for his almost aristocratic discretion. Here Borsani and Ponti discussed the inclination of the arms of a chair, whether angled upward as the former preferred or downward as the latter desired.

Today the villa, open to the public by appointment, maintains its markedly testimonial character as a creative achievement and a unique business model. It is a magnificent example, complete and perfectly preserved, of the relationship between architecture and interiors—and we cannot forget the emotional value that comes from the five generations that lived here until 2008, as so many episodes in a rare family history.

The door, by the artist Adriano Spilimbergo, separating the living room from the dining area, set on a raised level.

Previous pages:
The living room on the side facing the garden with a card table and period handcrafted curtains.

Detail of the mantelpiece and fireplace by Lucio Fontana with the title and theme Battaglia. On the right, a complete view with wall light fixtures by Guglielmo Ulrich to the sides; and the P40 armchair.

Following pages:
The bar in the gameroom with a painting by Luca Crippa and, among the details, the AT16 coat stand. Gaetano's bedroom, later Fulgenzio's, with colors and period furnishings, including an elegant dressing table.

CASA
QUARESTA

CASA QUARESTANI

ETTORE SOTTSASS, MILAN, 1986

A home that epitomizes
the poetics of Ettore Sottsass:
vibrant, bright, ironic.
Without changing the masonry
structure, his language has
personalized the interiors.
From the color palette
to the bespoke furnishings,
his style, while complementing
the spaces, renders everything
unique.

The entryway is the epitome of Ettore Sottsass's poetics. From the ground floor rises a staircase covered—floor and walls—with mint green terrazzo tiles. At the top, a simple transparent double door defined by wooden surrounds, each painted in soft colors—pink, yellow, and blue—acts as a filter at the entrance.

Climbing the steps is like entering a small shrine, an initiatory path, a reminiscence of Indian cultures, a gesture that emphasizes the sacredness inherent to every architectural act.

"There is a magical rite," wrote Sottsass, "by which rain is invoked and propitiated by watering the dry dust of the earth. In the same way, the universe is invoked and propitiated by building a house."

Elena Quarestani, the founder of the Milanese multicultural venue Assab One devoted to contemporary art, is the owner and has lived here since the mid-1980s. The purchase of the early-twentieth-century building and the commission to Ettore Sottsass to restructure it and design the furniture dates to that time. The building is laid out on four floors, overlooking a residential street on one side and the deep garden at the back.

"It was not my first experience with him," says Quarestani. "For the previous house, when my former husband and I were very young, and our four children not yet born, we asked him for some suggestions. He predicted that we would not stay long in that house because the family would grow, so his work in it was restricted, just inventions rather than a real project. It was then that the bed that is still here was made."

Ettore Sottsass was a man of a thousand brilliant insights: his own, which he conveyed in writings, drawings, photographs, objects, and architecture, and those that he elicited from others.

His insights embraced a very broad spectrum. Stone walls, colors, lights, shadows, rituals, temples, India, ruins, Chinese ceramics, the Mediterranean, pop art, the underground press. Together they made up a vision of projects, of whatever nature—architecture, design, or graphics—that had at its core the existence of humanity and its search for relative happiness.

The insights of others arose from Sottsass being a natural seducer, with his writings, his drawings, and his thinking—highbrow without being academic; on the contrary, profoundly humanistic, capable of imagining utopias and speaking of emotions, archetypes, fears, nostalgia, eros, and insomnia while thinking about architecture. Over time, Sottsass became the maestro of numerous disciples, young designers, and architects, often from abroad, who in his studio—which became Sottsass Associati—sought for whatever one seeks from a guru. They then followed individual paths, often successfully. "We were so deeply influenced," says Michele De Lucchi, the closest of his young students at the time, "that we emulated him in everything: we wrote in capital letters like him, we ate in the same restaurants, we dressed like him."

Elena Quarestani recalls the names of the collaborators involved in both homes. In the first, George Sowden, Masanori Umeda, and the Japanese artist Tiger Tateishi, who created the pictorial decorations on the canopy bed designed by Sottsass. Of the second home she mentions the contributions of Marco Zanini, who hailed from Trentino like Sottsass and who studied in Florence in the days of radical design, Beppe Caturegli, and Giovannella Formica.

"Ettore's first words when he saw the house, and we still didn't know if he would accept the assignment, were 'Thank you for thinking of me.' In reality, it is I," says Quarestani, "who feel a sense of deep gratitude to him for offering me the experiences that are renewed daily by living here. He was a great gentleman, full of intense curiosity, attentive, and endowed with an intuitive intelligence, very generous with himself. I remember that several years after the end of the work he came one evening to dinner with Barbara Radice and, observing the bookcase he had designed, he became unhappy. He decided to replace it and designed a new one."

The architect endowed with light an interior that was originally quite dark by installing three fully glazed verandas in the living room, kitchen, and bedroom on the top floor. The alterations were not radical, "at the limit of our budget," notes Quarestani. Sottsass's hallmark, apart from the additional glazing, lay instead in the numerous custom-designed furnishings in the communal areas and those specifically devoted to each inhabitant. The bookcases and cupboards embedded in the niches, the handrails of the stairs, a short balustrade, a column faced with burl, the doors, the beds for the children's rooms—each different and special—the customized bathrooms. His language spread throughout the house without the masonry structure being greatly affected. Presences like fragments that distinguish the spaces while supporting them and bearing Sottsass's hallmarks: in the geometric patterns, in the colored elements, in the terrazzo tiles with sorbet colors covering portions of the floors and walls.

Ettore Sottsass was a great experimenter, a bearer of originality and discontinuity in the world of design, and his singular vision had accompanied him ever since his designs for Olivetti, where he began working in 1958. For the firm he designed the first large Elea 9003 computer and created the Valentine portable typewriter, an expression of anti-luxury, now mythical and invariably red. Sottsass traversed the collective experience of radical design

without renouncing his subjective vision; he was a founder of the Memphis group in 1981, triggering resounding upheaval in the world of design. Irreverent and very young, the members of the group launched a powerful cultural message. "Those designs, those drawings," writes Sottsass, "were attempts to present new intensity, to express more emotions, to convey more information, to use more aromas, to put more flavor into that design, because by then it tasted too much of cardboard." In 1985 he considered this experience over, more or less coinciding with the design of this home.

The numerous furnishings he designed in his lifetime are minor architectures, and his buildings, not many and mainly made together with Johanna Grawunder during the later part of his life, mostly came from a sum of volumes "that I can measure with the measurements of my body."

Sottsass has told us a lot about his personal life: his father, an architect from Trentino, the move to Turin, his studies, the initial difficulties in finding work, the terrible experience of the war. Chance and formative encounters, such as with the painter Luigi Spazzapan, and his love for Fernanda Pivano, his first wife, making him open to American culture. She was a translator and friend of major figures of the Beat generation. He discovered the charm of the American landscape, "the charm that the phantoms of the future always have." The Milan years, his long partnership and marriage with Barbara Radice, sharing travels and projects and founding the magazine *Terrazzo*. He has left a huge number of testimonies and documentary materials through which we can reconstruct

his achievements: magazines that he designed, drawings, ceramics, glass works, and furnishings that still live on in the homes of collectors. "Perhaps," he wrote, "this desire to leave traces of myself has also become an obsession that has been following me all my life." An obsession that reveals the need to counteract the impermanence of things and the imperfection of reality.

To this Milanese home Sottsass attributed a sense of rituality in the entryway, a joyful vibrancy that can be felt in the bright green kitchen, a touch of irony in the small temple resting on the ground and covering the fuse block, the pleasure of color in the elevator all pink on the inside, and the uniqueness of the bespoke furnishings, including the one to hold the clothes of the lady of the house in her dressing room: a solid and mysterious volume that has a space for everything. "My problem was and remains being able to design—if I can—honest and comfortable homes for my clients."

In the garden, which becomes almost a gallery, with a fountain by Andrea Branzi and an inscription on the wall by the artist Luca Pancrazzi, Ettore Sottsass left his mark with marble artifacts resembling archaeological finds: fragments of a pediment or tumuli on which to rest.

"I have always felt a special pleasure in photographing destruction. I have felt a special pleasure—always—in living slowly, mingling the destiny that silently leads me to destruction and that invades me with nostalgia, with the other destiny that instead leads me every day to recreate a fresh, new design, which tastes of chocolates, mints, and perhaps even lemons."

Previous pages:
The entryway with the Mini Mandala lamp by Johanna Grawunder and, on the ceiling, an installation by Federico Pietrella.

The living room, where Sottsass's intervention included new colors and materials. On the wall, a work by Tom Wesselmann.

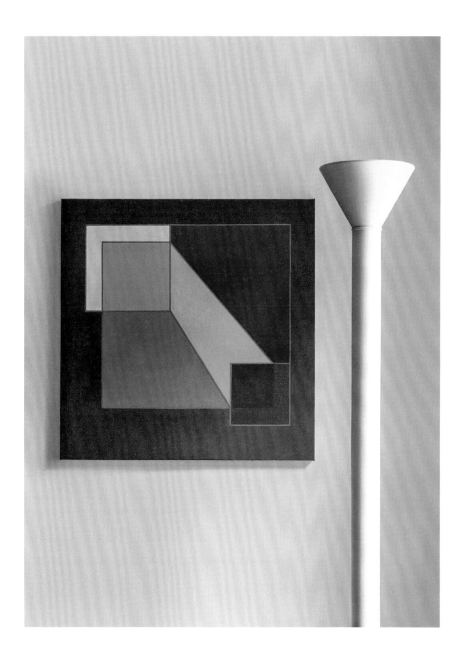

Colored geometries on the furniture designed by Sottsass and,
above, a work by Chung Eun-Mo.

CASA QUARESTANI

The custom-designed kitchen and, to the right, the dining area on the veranda with a table by Sottsass.

Following pages, on the left:
*Bedroom with the ZigZagZurich blanket by Nathalie Du Pasquier and George Sowden and silkscreen prints
by Andy Warhol.*
On the right: Among the details, in the stairwell, a family portrait by Cosimo Di Leo Ricatto.

Previous pages:
In the master bedroom, the bed is designed by Sottsass and painted by Tiger Tateishi;
the bedspread is by George Sowden and on the wall is a work by Remo Salvadori.

On the top floor the veranda opens fully onto the terrace and,
to the right, the designer storage unit in the master bedroom.

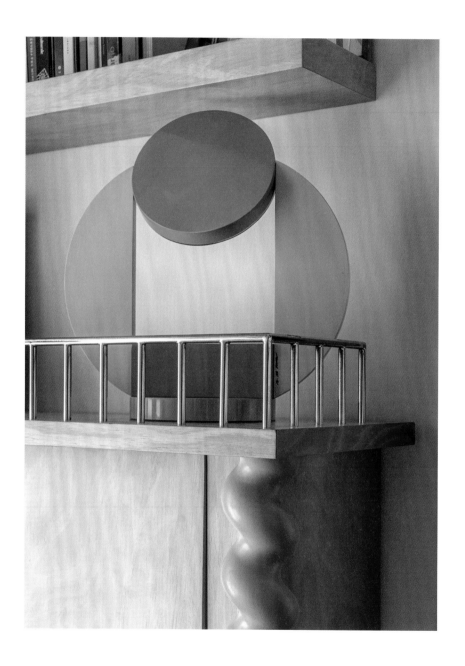

On a piece of furniture with recognizable details of Sottsass's work, a mirror from the Uno specchio per Donna limited series made by Gisella Borioli and Flavio Lucchini and, on the right, the customized wardrobe room.

VILLA
LA SCALA

VILLA LA SCALA

VITTORIANO VIGANÒ,
SAN FELICE DEL BENACO, 1956–1958

An encounter between an enlightened client and a bold architect gave rise to a building that combines the rough textures of concrete and stone and the immateriality of glass. With its minimalist silhouette, streamlined spaces, and transparent sliding windows, the home seems almost suspended in midair, an impression further accentuated by the dizzying flight of steps heading down to the lake.

Many consider La Scala the masterpiece of Vittoriano Viganò: a prominent Milanese architect of the post-war period, an important figure for all who study twentieth-century architecture, and a master who deserves to be better known by the general public.

La Scala is a villa on the slopes of Lake Garda (on the Brescia side), overlooking the Bay of Vento, not far from San Felice del Benaco. It was designed in 1956 and completed in 1958. The architectural quality that makes it exemplary is the outcome of the designer's experimental vision, matched by an extraordinary client: André Bloc—born in Algiers and painter, sculptor, engineer, publisher, and founder of the authoritative magazine *Architecture d'Aujourd'hui* for which Viganò became a correspondent.

The son of an architect, poet, and painter, Vittoriano Viganò immersed himself as a youth in Milanese culture, especially art. During those years he designed the premises of the Apollinaire, Schettini, Fiore, and Skyscraper galleries in Milan and participated in the activities of the Triennale. It was the tenth edition that made him stand out, with Pietro Porcinai, for a splendid and ephemeral aviary in the form of an inverted cone in nylon mesh.

Viganò embraced his professor Gio Ponti's ideas concerning color; in fact, Viganò became his assistant at the Milan Politecnico. He then joined the Concrete Art movement, which included the founders Gillo Dorfles and Bruno Munari, and took part in the Espace collective founded by Bloc himself with the goal of achieving a synthesis of the arts.

The villa was the result of the encounter between two different yet similar personalities: an architect who was a lover and connoisseur of art and an artist with an interest in architecture. If Viganò saw architecture as an artistic fact, Bloc created habitable sculptures that explored the interaction between the two disciplines.

In his impassioned lecture, delivered to mark the occasion of the centenary of Viganò's birth, Paolo Portoghesi recalls that *Architecture d'Aujourd'hui* was then the most popular architecture magazine and André Bloc, a well-known, sensitive, and great sculptor, could have entrusted the task to any other architect who was more famous and more experienced. In commissioning Viganò, states Portoghesi, "he knew he was dealing with a person of great culture, capable of establishing a very intense relationship between architecture and landscape by contrasting the image of the lake with a floating platform apparently exempt from the force of gravity."

La Scala is a building that expresses a complex rationality from a structural point of view and compares the materiality of reinforced concrete with the transparency of glass. The visitor perceives it as a refined glass box cantilevered out over a precipice, an observation deck surrounded by nature and projected toward the water and the sky.

The villa consists of two trapezoidal slabs in reinforced concrete: the first is the roof slab and the second is the base that supports the entire building in overhang above the lake. It does not rest on the ground, but is supported by a long concrete beam resting on H-shaped metal pillars. A system of sliding windows, opening in various ways, creates a continuous facade for constant sightlines with the lake and the garden. When the doors and windows are open, the separation between interior and exterior is erased and the relationship with nature is particularly profound.

The ground floor is a continuous space with minimal internal partitions—only three walls isolate the kitchen, bathroom, and guest room. Everything else is transparent. A sliding window separates the large living room from the portion that was once the bedroom and is now used as a dining room. The lowest part of the building, which was André Bloc's atelier, hosts a bedroom.

The name of the villa derives from another astonishing feature of the design: the dizzying 130-foot-long staircase leading from the home down to the landing stage. It is supported by a concrete girder: ninety steps of sheet iron that in the casting phase were inserted into the concrete and bent to form the parapet. Consisting of the treads alone, almost accentuating the sense of suspension of the descent, they cover a difference in altitude of 150 feet. At the end of the path that winds between the trees, the long jetty, without any protection, enters the water supported by seven pillars. It is an architectural promenade devoted to nature, an emotional path that projects the gaze downward, an offspring of the home that emphasizes its bold design. Today, the trees are much leafier than in the past, enveloping the steps and camouflaging its design which, very visible in the photos when the building was still recent, is an impressive sloping line, a bold and decisive gesture.

The expressiveness of reinforced concrete and its rough and imprecise material, here set in contrast to the glass, form the stylistic hallmark of Vittoriano Viganò's designs.

During the time he was working on La Scala, he also designed the building that catapulted him onto the international scene. This was the Istituto Marchiondi Spagliardi in the Baggio district in Milan, intended to host troubled young people. It was a kind of reformatory that Viganò undertook with new pedagogical criteria, abolishing all barriers and proposing spaces that could awaken in the residents a sense of self-awareness and freedom. "At the time," recalls Paolo Portoghesi, "they were called 'houses of correction' and abandoning this name already showed the innovative intentions of the architect and his clients

Previous pages:
View of the living room.

Details of the Verona stone slabs that emerge from the fireplace to become seats;
a metal sculpture by André Bloc.

. . . Bruno Zevi, commenting on the work in *Espresso*, chose as always a brilliant headline, 'The Boys Don't Run Away.'" Built in reinforced concrete, it was described by Reyner Banham in his *The New Brutalism. Ethic or Aesthetic* as "one of the greatest surprises of European architecture," calling it realistic and unsentimental. Today, the building is in a condition of dramatic abandonment and, as Franz Graf wrote, "the 'extremist' complex at the time of its conception is in a state of equally 'extreme' decay."

La Scala is also well suited to the brutalist vocabulary, a term that does not exhaust its expressiveness and of which Viganò offered his own personal interpretation, speaking of "brutalism as the recognition of the value (formal and civil) of modest materials; brutalism: as a challenge to the elegant, easy, elite attitude; brutalism: as the assumption of unified material tools, interior/exterior, and simplification."

As if to soften the severity and hardness of concrete, in his buildings and interior designs the use of color is very important—not as a decorative presence, but rather as part of the structure itself. Red, above all, was accompanied by blue or black. The first became a sign of identity, from Marchiondi to the School of Architecture at the Milan Politecnico, whose expansion Viganò worked on starting in the 1970s and which he distinguished with a great crimson-red A (for Architecture, Asymmetry, Amor).

At La Scala the color was originally more intense than it is today: the plaster of the living room ceiling had blue and red parts; the pillars were black and red; the windows were shielded by red and gray Venetian blinds; and the walls were painted blue. In the late 1960s, when André Bloc died, the home was sold and the new owners decided to leave it basically unchanged. A monumental fireplace designed by Maurizio Betta was added to the living room, which developed around a series of Verona stone slabs that can also be used as seating. Viganò frequented the home even after the alterations that followed the change of ownership and did not disapprove of them.

For many years, the Milanese architect had been a professor, or rather a "master," as many students called him. The Amor alluded to by the letter A on the facade of the School is reserved for Architecture, a discipline to which he devoted himself with intense passion throughout his life. He designed very elegant furnishings and light fixtures, some of which have been reissued today. In fact, they made a profound impression when he was a technical-artistic consultant for ArteLuce, the company founded by Gino Sarfatti. His international outlook was expressed in his constant knowledge of and dealings with architects from other countries.

In his practice, he found space for poetry, materials, solutions, and colors. Bob Noorda recalls that "toward the end of his life, he never used a pencil, but only a red marker and a black one, and he made beautiful drawings. He was a great poet. His work was a work of poetry."

Here, on the shores of the lake, Viganò exalted the architectural devices in relation to the landscape without indulging in sentimentality. He proposed a refined way of living and established vibrant relationships between environment, architecture, and art. Originally, the interior housed numerous sculptures made by Bloc, which found an exceptional setting against the backdrop of the lake and contributed to that bond between the arts that united architect and client.

Glass and stone are the protagonists also in the dining room.

The bathroom is clad with porphyroid slabs, like the continuous floors of the villa.

Following pages:
The exterior facing the garden shows the elements composing the building:
a glass volume set between two concrete slabs.

*The expressiveness of the concrete and, on the right and on the following page, the metal pillars reveal
the distinctive features of the brutalist language.*

Following pages:
Two details of the long and stunning flight of steps descending to the lake.

Cover
Museo Casa Mollino, detail of the living room
Back Cover
Casa Fornasetti, detail of the music room
p. 1
Villa Borsani, detail of the living room
pp. 2–3
Casa Mendini, detail of the bedroom
p. 4
Casa Quarestani, detail of a piece of furniture

Concept and Texts
Chiara Dal Canto

Photographs
Lorenzo Pennati

Translation
Richard Sadleir

Editorial Project
Valentina Lindon

Art Direction and Graphic Design
Cristina Menotti

© 2023 Mondadori Libri S.p.A.

Distributed in English throughout the World
by Rizzoli International Publications Inc.
300 Park Avenue South
New York, NY 10010, USA

ISBN 978-88-918354-1-3

2023 2024 2025 2026 / 10 9 8 7 6 5 4 3 2 1

First edition: March 2023

This volume was printed at
L.E.G.O. S.p.A., Vicenza
Printed in Italy

Visit us online:
Facebook.com/RizzoliNewYork
Twitter: @Rizzoli_Books
Instagram.com/RizzoliBooks
Pinterest.com/RizzoliBooks
Youtube.com/user/RizzoliNY

ACKNOWLEDGMENTS
The authors thank
Francesca Prina
for her careful attention
to the texts.

Archivio Gae Aulenti,
Archivio Osvaldo Borsani,
Archivio Gabriella Crespi,
Nina Artioli,
Elisabetta Crespi,
Josef Dalle Nogare,
Tommaso Fantoni,
Fulvio Ferrari,
Barnaba Fornasetti,
Roberto Gigliotti,
Elisa and Fulvia Mendini,
Elena Quarestani,
Barbara Radice,
Augusto Righi,
Francesca Riva,
and the Vergani family.

Chiara Dal Canto would
personally like to thank
Luciano Giorgi.

Thanks also to the following for
assistance with the photographs:
Simone Fico,
Riccardo Giancola,
Nicola Milla,
Alice Traballi,
Susanna Zini.
Special thanks to Ilaria Franza for
her constant support and untiring
enthusiasm.